I0098887

A Melody of Memories

A Melody of Memories

A Poetry Book

by

Donna Antonacci

Streets of Honor Publishing, New York

A MELODY OF MEMORIES

Printing History
Published by Streets of Honor Publishing
First Edition/April 2011
All rights reserved.
Copyright © 2011 by Donna Antonacci

(Editing, done by Chicago Manual of Style editing standards)

No parts of the work may be reproduced or transmitted in any form or by any means, electronic or mechanical, including photocopying and recording, or by any information storage or retrieval system, except as may be expressly permitted in writing from the Publisher. For information address:
Streets of Honor Publishing, PO Box 931 Mohegan Lake, New York 10547

http://www.streetsofhonor.com or e-mail streetsofhonor@aol.com

For more info and pictures on A MELODY OF MEMORIES

http://www.amelody of memories.com

ISBN (13) = 978-0-9786760-5-6

PRINTED IN THE UNITED STATES OF AMERICA

Acknowledgments

To my children: Danielle, Joey, and Mike—for your love and keeping my heart filled with joy always

To my granddaughter Alana, who is my most precious treasure

To Al—for your love, support, and for believing in me

To my extended family members including my close friends: thank you all for your encouragement

To my publisher, Streets of Honor Publishing—for helping me get this book out to the market the right way

To my editor and friend, author Stephen A. Welles—for your knowledge, wisdom, and superior guidance

CONTENTS

From the heart of the matter...

A Gift of my heart

I won't reject you

I pray my body accepts you

I waited for you for a long time

A chance for life

You will forever be a part of me

Someone died that I might have you

How brave that person was

How caring, loving and pure

Will we be compatible

I'm not afraid, I welcome you

My body is a chalice

This new heart, my blood
Precious heart beat inside me

Forever and forever

A Mom

You are so sick,
but a tiny voice calls out in the night,
and you rush to rescue

You are so hungry,
but there aren't enough pork chops
so you pass

You are so worried about money
but you never let on

You are so sad,
but you smile and laugh
and make it believable

You are so lonely,
but their hugs help to fill the void

You are so overwhelmed,
but you keep taking on more

You are so scared,
but you try to be the bravest person they know

You are so doubtful,
but you remain the most positive
person they know

You are fragile; you look into the sky,
keep on praying and never question why

A Mother's Prayer

In time I will grow old and gray,
remember to have patience with me
Long ago I had patience and helped you grow

When I can't remember anymore, help me
think it through
remember when you were small, I was
there for you

If the time comes that I can no longer speak,
just sit by me and hold my hand

If my legs no longer work,
lend me your hand as I did when you
took your first step

When I close my eyes and take my last breath,
try to remember that we both did our best

An Angel's Voice

Softly she came to me
In my dreams I felt her wings touch me
Her voice gentle, I see a reflection,
her slight existence reassures me

She flew down from a cloud
Sat with me only a moment
I long to feel her surround me
Swipe my mind with all her glory

Fly past the moon and the sun
Blink away the light and warmth of the day
Your breath so sweet like honey cups
Your golden hair a silky glaze

Come to me in dreams once more
Take my mind inside myself
Deep inside a place untouched
Visit me again, you must

A New Day

The tick of the clock echoes in my ear
Birds chirp and I know day is here

Stretch away the ache inside me
Feel the cool air rise and guide me

A new day has begun
The trees bend and bounce back like me

Resilient in every thought inside me
Making way for a new beginning

Market my ideas, choices never fears
Success stands before me

Break down the wall of old feelings
Support your inner being

You are the one who molds the future
Be strong within yourself always

Anticipation

No words can tell my desire
dream on to a place much higher

Your lips on mine feel warm
your arms secure and strong

Time is passing much too slow
pack my bags together we go

Together once more our time will be
special, tender, young and free

Bob and Barb

You touched my heart a million miles
Many years ago

Skating by and cycle dust
Together we would go

Time has passed behind us now
The quiet settled in

I miss the man who touched my heart
I still remember when

Your quiet, sweet and gentle ways
Have never left my side

But now your pace has mellowed dear
Inside alone I cry

My love for you will never die
I only wish you could

Carry me back to the days
Of whispers understood

When we fall asleep at night
I thank the Lord above

For all our years together
You are my one true love

Broken Promise

I didn't want to leave you here,
Please don't fade away my dear

I sit with you each day
And whisper that you might remember

Do you feel me by your side,
Stroking you with loving pride

Your mind was strong, your body firm,
Your flowing hair, your loving charm

You would dance into my arms,
I miss the days that are now gone

I promise not to put you here,
Please forgive me could you dear

I hate to leave you every day
Returning home alone and pray

I wish that I could carry you far away
And start brand new

Our tired bodies are now old,
I can no longer take the cold

I promised not to put you here,
The nurse is calling please don't fear

Your children love you, so do I,
Rest my darling, please don't cry

Butterfly

A butterfly with injured wing
Lay upon my deck

I cradled it and wonder how
The children felt its depth

Repairing love healed into night
By morning butterfly took flight

It flew away
Then made a turn

Flew back to me
To show concern

Thank you it fluttered
I wish you knew

Without my wings
I'd never do

By the Sea

I sit by our favorite spot by the crystal sea
Waves clash against the rocks like poetry

My thoughts awaken and I write
My feelings of you and my life

A journey that has been so grand
Love, children, family's helping hand

I close my eyes and reminisce
Of happy times, a younger miss

Simple things glowed like the sun
A wedding, a birth, a job well done

Listen to the seagull's call
Dancing on the ocean's floor

A rainbow streams across the sea
Like diamonds that you once gave me

This special place for me to rest
The perfect sea, I'm Heaven's guest

Cancer

I don't fear you

It was just a matter of time
Before you might visit

It was only a question of when
And how I would accept you

I won't let you command me,
I'm too smart for that

I will continue to work, to dance,
To smile and to love

If I find time,
I might pray for you to go away

I won't run to God for answers,
He wouldn't give what I can't handle

I can do this, take the pain,
The worry, the uncertainty, but
I won't fear you

When it's over and you disappear,
I'll be grateful

I won't invite you back to visit
I may make the time to pray just a little more

Central Park

800 acres, a welcome oasis
Sit by a lake in the warm summer air

Skate on a rink in the cold not a care
Fountains that spout like a whale at sea

Children at play feeding pigeons so free
Sit in a boat and glide right by,
attractions of baseball, tennis, birds fly.

Relax, socialize, meditate too
a feeling for everyone, including you
Thousands of trees that dance in the breeze
A zoo for the children to learn and to grow -

A carousel of colors in the summer glow,
always on the go

20 million people a year make a trip to be,
in Central Park a place to feel free

Christmas

Feel the chill a time of thrill
rejoice and sings, what Christmas brings

Santa, toys, choir boys
pretty things, angel's wings

Shoppers rush here and there
some of us without a care

Jingle bells, cocoa smell, candy canes, and
cookie trains
feel the feeling you know so well

Wish for this, giving that
peace on earth, can't package that

Children's eyes with surprise
memories of years gone by

Hearts together once a year
wish the feeling would endear

Each and every day could be
a perfect world for you and me

Complain

It's too hot, it's too cold
Wish I were young, I'm getting old

I'm too fat, I'm too thin
Pluck a hair from my chin

Taxes up, jobs are gone
Acid rain, polluted farm

Wedlock doesn't rock no more
Decree divorce with certainty

Vote for him, or her or it
Praying later they would quit

Respect the president and priest
Deception has become a feast

Break the rules, break your back
Everything just seems offtrack

Cornucopia

Family - so many memories

Friendship - so many gifts

Love - so much joy

Pain - so much growth

Money - so many choices

Talent - so many opportunities

Sickness - so much courage

Kisses - so much healing

Death - so many farewells

Daddy's Girl

As she stood before me in all her wonder,
I promised myself to hold back the tears

How precious my little girl looked.

I remember the first day I held her in my arms,
So innocent, so small. I promised God I would
protect her forever.

The white lace and beads on her gown
Reflected against the stained glass
windows of the church

As the organist played Ave Maria, everyone stood
And tears fell from my wife's eyes

We proceeded down the aisle savoring each step,
Knowing that she would soon belong to him

I lifted her veil, gave her a gentle kiss
As my heart swelled with pride

She took his hand and I wiped a tear
from my cheek and
Said goodbye to my little girl

Dance with Me

Minuet with me my prince
Fitted in my gown of silk and beads

Twirl me in circles roundabout
Posture perfect pair are we

In my glory, every step
Press my bosom to your chest

Music, madness, masterpiece
A venue for all eyes to feast

Dancing through the night till dawn
Every step a star reborn

Deeply gaze into my eyes
Connected wearing no disguise

Dance with me into the night
Dance with me and hold me tight

Dance

Shuffle your feet to so many beats

Rumba and sway like a snake at play

Samba and glide your feet collide

Waltz through the air without a care

Swing and twist like a lindy gist

Salsa your hips to a sexy mix

Hustle around like a diva would do

Cha-cha and shake and begin to create

Merengue around to a Latin sound

Quick Step and run to a beat like none

Tango so close with passion engrossed

Darn Car

Ching, ching
There goes my bling, bling

Another tune-up, calendar shows
Timing belt, transmission and new hose

Rotate those tires
New fan belt

Steering fluid and antifreeze
Money flying like the breeze

Rotors, brakes, inspection due
Fuel injection service too

Wheel alignment, ac broke
Computer diagnostics, what a joke

Towing, jump start, oil change
Shocks and struts, it's such a shame

Clutches, radiator, carburetor too
Just end it all, collision due

Day and Night

Did you hear my heart beat?
Hear the rhythm so sweet

Only you can move me right
Into the night

Hold your body to mine, feeling free and easy,
Touch me deep forever, never, never leave me

Mark my soul forever, magic man you thrill me.
Longing makes it sweeter, taste my tenderness

How can we forget, the moments that we met,
Magnets in the night, bound to you in flight

Touch my heart so deeply, feeling never
leaves me,
Return to me forever, satisfy my needs

We should never vanish, the picture is so clear,
You and I together our future is clear

Did You Ever Hear Me?

I held you tight
Morning, noon and night

I prayed that life
would be kind to you

I hoped you would have
more opportunity than me

I watched you blossom
into a precious rose

I hoped you would look
to me as your rock

I observed your steps
always praying you would
take the right path

I dried your tears
Each time a piece of my
heart chipped away

I would speak of your beauty
Little did you know how deep
your beauty really was

I would feel so proud
I felt no other mother could
feel the way I do

I said "I love you" a million times
Did you ever hear me?

Dreams

Once in a dream I sat with you
A magical place just meant for two

Our spirits tied tight like delicate twigs
Burning bonfire a warmth so big

A peaceful place by a trickling stream
Sat upon rocks and shared our dreams

Hear a dream melody, violin strings
Echo a tune of lovers in spring

Cherish your dreams, those understood
Treasures of mind and all things good

Enchanted night of dark then dawn
Each vision waiting to be born

Hold on to your dreams when you awake
Hold close to your heart for heaven's sake

Empty

I feel like a prisoner,
I feel no love in here

My insides scream for air,
my heart aches for comfort

Days here are long,
nights are empty and cold

The future seems grim
no plans or final reassurance

Nobody really hears or sees me
go through the motions no end in sight

Does anybody really care?
they say, be grateful for what you have

They don't understand
my heart is empty
for a very, very long time

Feelings

My love, feel my heart beat like a drum
echoing into the night

My desire so strong, pressed tightly together
like a bunch of sweet lilacs

I dream of you each evening,
rock me in slumber in a sea of blankets

I walk in motion
with life only to return to my destination

Your arms safe and warm,
where I belong two hearts one song

Fiery Red Tango Shoes

A proper Milonga is all I need
dance close, embrace, let the man lead

Ocho in sync, pivot and trace
my slim body dressed in lace

Our eyes affixed, a Latin stare
hair slicked back without a care

Together in passion, our bodies are one
Breast to chest, cheek to tongue

Sensual combo of kicks and sways
artwork form for all to praise

Glide by people who stop and stare
my fiery red tango shoes take me there

Fly Away

The time has come, he couldn't stay
Must spread his wings, he's on his way

Destination hope and doubt
I see strength, his insides shout

Goodbye to days of Candy Land
A young man stands, a reaching hand

Raised with love and tender care
My child, my boy of golden hair

Your mother I will always be
Now I step back and set you free

Friendship

Can I tell you how I feel?

That my insides ache

I want to scream for real

You are always there to listen

If I tell you the truth, you just grin

When I curse you say it's not a sin

You are tough with me because you care

Then as gentle as the summer air

You never tire when my stories drag on

What about you do I hear your song?

The years are passing and we've grown so close

When I joke your smile is so sweet

If my heart is breaking, I feel your stroke

My friend you are always there

I love that I need you, want to share

On the day that you are gone

Your strength will help me carry on

Going Nowhere Fast

Fly birds, cars, people
jetting by, going nowhere fast

Hurry, hurry, catch a train
Is it all in vain

The wind is blowing, the race is on
Catch a falling star

The wind is storming, furious and fast
No one grounded, going nowhere fast

Scent of roses, blow in the breeze
Garden hoses, water running free

Run the track and pound the earth
What is it all really worth

Going nowhere fast
How much longer can we last

Gossip

Gossip, greedy, ghoulish talk, the kind
that women spew
Talk that hurts your feelings, talk that isn't true

Rip into a young girl's heart, a reputation hurt
Saying that she's this and that, just
a constant flirt

Why do women do this? Such a painful game
Such a waste of energy, what is there to gain?

If they were on the other end, attacking
you inside
So much better that you live with a sense of pride

Insecure, weak followers, time that they grew up
Stand beside each other and time that
they shut up

Remember we are women, mothers,
and sisters too
That we need each other, sometimes a
man won't do

So keep these thoughts in mind, review them day
and night
Always treat each other, in a way that's right

Grandmother

Teach me all I need to know
Through the years and watch me grow

You cradled me and kept me safe
With love, a tender, warm embrace

You would listen carefully
Never judge, made me feel free

You would sigh with sheer delight
Then sit with me into the night

Read fairy tales of Jack and Jill
Laugh and hug, our hearts would spill

Your warm hugs would keep me strong
Always teaching right from wrong

Someday you'll watch me from above
And I will always feel your love

Hair

I adore my hair
It goes with me everywhere

Updo, Pageboy, Bouffant, a Bob,
Bangs on top will do the job

Hang to my waist Rapunzel style,
Sinead O'Connor's buzz is wild

Hair can hide your ears
It can also hide your fears
Staying with you for years

My hair dances as I walk
Through the breeze hear my hair talk

As it sits upon my crown
Shining princess will astound

Extra weight I would not trade
My hair, my pride, I've got it made

Happy Thoughts

Happiness is a cup of herbal tea
Or when your grandchild sits upon your knee

The telephone rings on a lonely night
A friend calls to say let's go for a bite

At work you're sad and the boss would say
What a great job you did today

You diet and diet but the pounds won't budge
A friend knocks at your door with diet fudge

Outside it's raining cats and dogs
Inside you play with puppy paws

Your x-ray comes back not looking clear
Your husband says "don't worry dear".

You watch while couples dance with ease
A dance host pulls you to your knees

Years pass, you wait for Mr. Right
You bump into him on Saturday night

For all the HAPPY THOUGHTS I feel
They all turn out to be so real

His Love

Ladies only know when a man takes
hold of your soul you can't let go

Have you ever been in love?
feel like you could touch the moon's smiling face

The longing pains more than the deepest cut
and the healing only comes with his touch

The hunger and emptiness linger on
until the moment that you can
feel his nourishment

Be where you are yet
feel so detached, so distant, so displaced

Life must go on, play the game,
remain the same, can't break these chains,
no gain just pain

His Eyes

He touches my face, traces it with his tiny hands
If he could only see the love in my eyes as I watch
him sleep
Does he realize what he'll miss
the raindrops, the setting of the sun
the moon's happy face

So innocent, each day passes like another
full of energy he trips and falls.
He jumps to his knee, his smile like a
raging bonfire, so determined to try again

Does he realize what he'll miss,
the fireworks, the Christmas lights
and bunny eggs.

His ears will lead him, his touch will guide him
and someday his best friend the canine
will direct him!

My little boy I wish you could
see my face, my smile and the love I feel for you.

Wish I could share my eyes with you,
see me wink, stick out my tongue
as we make funny faces.

My heart swells when I see how hard
you try to do your best.

My child we look the same,
our hazel eyes, our golden hair,
that tiny dimple we both share

We are both determined, strong,
we will survive, take my hand,
you are safe with me.

I Remember

I'm sitting all alone today by my favorite rock
Looking back at my life in my favorite park

I remember my childhood playing with free will
Skate along the sidewalk, jump rope,
Jack and Jill

School days filled with dancing and that
favorite boy
Friends forever, yearbook, laughing, tears of joy

When I fell in love with that special man
When he placed a diamond gently on my hand

The birth of my first child, proud as I could be
When I held her in my arms my life had harmony

My life is slowing ending, the final chapter near
So many blessing came to me, throughout
each passing year

My mind holds no regrets
No sadness in my heart

I'm grateful for each moment
From the very start

I Wonder

Did she dream when she was young
Of a daughter or a son

Did she wonder what would be
A home, a husband, maybe me

Was she pretty, running free,
Singing songs and climbing trees

Did she hope to grow and be
A perfect lady, smart and free

Did love hurt her more than once
Or did she feel love a whole bunch

I wonder if all her dreams came true
Someday I'll ask her

I Believe in You

So sweet to love someone
You give the perfect care

Longing for the next day
To touch her golden hair

Dance across the moonlight
Touch a falling star

Hear the echo chiming
Like strings on a guitar

Pray that life continues
Would hate to see it end

Believing in each other
My lover and my friend

If I Were

If I were a horse I would gallop all day
and just eat hay

If I were a cow I would give milk all day
and still find time to pray

If I were a bird I would fly through the sky
and wave goodbye

If I were a snail I would crawl in the rain
and never refrain

If I were a snake I would slither around
and never frown

If I were a bee I would think of honey
down by the tree

If I were a chicken I would cluck and cluck
and wish myself luck

If I were a donkey I wouldn't fret
I would think I were funky

If I were a cat fluffy and smooth
It would put me in a good mood

But I'M A PIG, I belong in the mud
and I feel like crud

If I Could Fly

I would soar to the moon
and place your face upon it
for the world to see you smile

I would fly with every seagull
over mighty shores
and sprinkle tiny kisses
on sand castles galore

Above a cloud is where I'd go
and shout so God would hear
I fell in love the moment
her smile was oh so clear

Over lakes and rivers
crystal blue delight
I would fly the distance
and hold you through the night

In My Dreams

My dreams are busting at the seams
Think of you and let out screams

Never knew what could have been
Would you trade, sit in the shade
Could have had it made

Sorry not easy to say
In my dreams watch me pray
The sky no longer gray

In my dreams I read your mind
You cheated me blind

Miss my brown eyes, give a wave
Standing sole before my grave

In my dreams, all that I see
My love, my life, my destiny

Inside Myself

My body shakes at night

And then when I awake

Will I ever feel content

Inside my heart still breaks

I want to shout aloud

For the world to hear

I write the poems for all to read

Not knowing it's my plea

I cannot feel the love

No matter how I try

Entangled bodies soothe my soul

Then I come home to cry

What will be my destiny?

Live my life, I must love me

Jealousy

It's no secret
Maybe a sin

I can't hide
What I feel within

A fire, a burning
Inside my heart

I feel no anger, only fear
A threat, a suspicion, seems so clear

Negative feelings hamper me
Pass from doubt to certainty

A smiling enemy by my side
Very cunning, not contrite

Like a poison in my veins
Secrecy that has no shame

Knowing well
That he's to blame

Jersey Man

He came from nowhere,
takes my hand, my heart, feels right

Touch me gently
to a place no man has been, it is not a sin

Allows me to be me,
he sets me free

Sing and laugh into the night
no time to fight

Love and listen all we say
always finding time to play

Just being who we are,
a gift to each other near or far

Joey

Middle son of mine
stuck between one sweet, one keen

Kind and strong and deep at times
feelings kept inside a heart so wide

Look at him and you can see
his grandfather's face dark and lean

Busy son, having fun, running here running there
dreams to be so great one day

Pray your dream come true your way
special man to all you touch

Heart of gold and Midas touch
always in my heart and soul
proud to be the Mom God chose.

Josie

My sweet friend of yesterday,
strangers that fit so well

Years between us yet connected
like a pair of precious stones

Instant like and fondness grew
enjoying friendship always true

The ache of life made you strong
kept on going sang your song

We can laugh into the day
always knowing what to say

Years are passing, hold on tight
always loving, never fight

Now we're older and I'm glad
all moments we have shared

And for you I'll always wish
that God bless you with a kiss

You are special, kind and true
my dear Josie, I LOVE YOU

Judging

Don't judge me by my cover
My mind is broad and fair

Don't judge me by my color
A rainbow doesn't care

Don't judge me by my voice
An ugly bird sings sweet

Don't judge me by my age
My wisdom can defeat

Don't judge me by my money
It won't buy you love

Only one can judge me
That is God above

Just for You

If I could reach the sky,
I would steal each star for you

The moon would reflect your smile,
and would be smiling for two

I would blow a tune so sweet,
the light would shine a magic beat

Young and free in love we are,
even though we're from afar

Laughter

Laughter is music, sunshine and rain
Laughter the cure for all your pain

A smile, the joy, a wish, a grin
Laughter can wash away all your sin

A cheerful sound that will astound
A giggling babe, the sound we crave

Laughter is long, laughter is short
A belly laugh that will make you snort

Laugh away pain, laugh away loss
Laugh away words of a nasty boss

Laugh until there is nothing left
Laughter will make you feel your best

Little Angels

They sit on candy clouds
Naked bottoms, innocent miracles

Angelic faces, rainbow of colors
Broken promises, shattered dreams

They float on rivers of tears
Young mother's pine for years

Empty arms ache
Powdered scented candles fill the air

Sweet angels, sleep in heaven
Cradled by God's love

Knitting needle placed aside
Baby booties, swaddling cloths,
again I cry

Be strong they say
Not meant to be

My precious baby
Taken from me

Looking Down

Can you feel a tear fall from the sky

So sad to see my people die

From war, sickness, anger, fear

God's creations fading here

The flowers, tree, oceans too

Plant a seed for me and you

The seed of love is what we need

Selfish, greedy we've become

Hate and anger on the run

Nations plot to end the day

The final curtain, we all pay

No need to fear

We'll all be done

No more tears

We'll all be gone

Love Letters

I store them in a secret place only for my eyes
Your sentiment, your sweet refrain, our
laughter and our cries

Each and every letter a token from your heart
They sit upon each other a collection
from our start

All these letters written in the perfect tone
Your took the time to do this just for me alone

The first day that we met and all
the days to come
We walk the beach together with the setting sun

The kisses you have given tender, always sweet
All the tears that you have dried
helping me defeat

All of my collection, a set of perfect poems
They sit upon my heart, gentle to the bone

Your words have kept me strong, the
beauty of your love
Your letters keep us bonded, sweet letters of love

Love Reunion

Children of the past,
once touched by stolen moments

Our lives separate,
but memories of yesterday still linger on

Although apart,
inside our minds and hearts
each reserve room for our return

Wondering, waiting,
what magnetism binds our thoughts together?

Would they return to fill the emptiness, the desire?
the undying want that only they remember

Out of nowhere,
joined together once more

A second chance for happiness,
two smiles of long ago

Two hearts rejoined,
two hands touch once more

No words are needed
these two know what was once shared
time has not destroyed

Maybe Next Time

She tried her best to get the part
Did she touch your heart

A voice of an angel, moves like a dove
Acts, like a pro, scenes of love

She tried her best to impress the crowd
She would twirl, and echo right out loud

Flying like an eagle, spinning like a top
Competing, like a champ, never time to stop

She would never falter, always kept her smile
Chin held high, could almost touch the sky

Stronger than the ocean, she would start again
Always keep in mind losing's not a sin

Memories

Hold on to them deep inside,
close your eyes, feel them come alive

No one can shatter, tarnish or burn
your memories will always return

The smell, the touch, the taste,
his eyes, tells it all, full recall

Never lonely, a state of mind
your memories, your company, surreal, divine

A tear may fall, your strength be there
for memories your heart can always share

Michael

He moves like lightning
young and free

His eyes are eager so carefree
many feelings deep inside
very silent child of mine

Funny, freaky comic boy
makes me laugh with so much joy

Tries so hard to do his best,
never taking time to rest

Sometimes silly, makes me laugh
forget your problems what a blast

Hopes and dreams deep down inside
of NBA and slam dunk pride

Whatever be, I pray for you
may God decide your dreams come true

Missing Him

He comes and goes busy breadwinner

Involved in work, community and secret places

She waits patiently for his return

Close your eyes and feel his strength around you

Sleep in an empty bed and imagine
him inside you

His passion carries you through the day

You drink alone without the clink of glasses

Counting the clock with passing hours

Waiting to share your stories and adventures

He's closer now, he'll break me in his grasp

We will pass the night in a sea of blankets

Loving until the next time he leaves me

Missing You

He still tugs on my heart
they say move on to a better place

When I see a rose, I think of the first
time he gave me mine

As I sit on the beach I hear your
sweet whispers in my ear

When I stroll down the street
its your hand I'm missing

He dances with me now but
it's your lead I'm longing for

In the evening when I dine
I watch the candle burn and see your reflection

As we lay in bed at night and he
touches me I still feel you inside me

They say move on to a better place
but I only think of you

Money

The root of all evil some would say
While others rush to get their pay

Money can change you life indeed
For some their life can turn to greed

Some say it's precious, money is power
It serves no good at your final hour

Money gives sparkle, like diamonds and trips
Lavish food that goes to your hips

Money makes people lie and deceive
How much money do you really need

Money is war, money is pain
Destruction of nations, medium of exchange

Money can't buy life
Money can't buy time
Money can't buy wisdom
Money can't buy love

My Child

I dreamt of you before you arrived

I loved you before I knew who you would be

I could feel you move inside me

You continued to grow and being a woman
never felt better

As my body changed, we grew closer and closer

Your shape was more evident and my heart
swelled with pride

I took care, was patient and prepared for your
grand arrival

When our eyes first met, I knew God existed

When I held you in my arms I was blessed
for a lifetime

My Love

Apart from you my time spent is incomplete
but memories of our last encounter keep me alive

Dreaming of being together again, alone,
feeling,
sharing special things, secret things

My Love, only you can read my silent moments,
only you can understand my moods,
hopes and dreams

To imagine life without you is to not take breath
to be locked away with no escape
to life's wonders

Together, we climb the mountain of life,
without you I fall

Together, we cross endless oceans,
without you I will drown

Together, we are one,
without you I am not yet born

Pass life with me, always close by,
for as long as long is

My Most Precious me

I could share a recipe
A story, tell a joke for free

I might share a poem with you
A verse that's sad or make you glad

I could teach you all my tricks
An exercise, a body fix

Dance with me and you will learn
Passion in a rhythmic turn

Of all the precious things I share
Would it be a lock of hair

No, "my most precious me"
To give my heart entirely

One More Chance

I run to your hugs and safe arms
This is what I miss the most
I look up at your gaze and scratchy beard
that shadows me on a sunny day

I check your pocket for that special gift
a trinket that tells me I was in your thoughts
Your manly scent reminds me how
strong you are
How hard you work for me each day

You are the best man I've known
The one who made me feel like a princess
One more chance to sit by you
This is what my heart misses

Your picture sits by my bed
Your smiling face and dimples like mine
Daddy why are you gone
My memories will go on

One more chance to share a play
One more chance, I dream each day

On My Own

It's not so bad a single plate
sitting home without a date

Shopping easy small amounts
watching television on the couch

Lots of room to hang my clothes
no complaints from my pantyhose

Cooking is a cinch these days
no big meals and pans to scrape

The dust can sit and linger too
no need to impress it's only you

Now I read in silence here
no confusion, no dog hair

When I slip inside my sheets
this is when I skip a beat

I miss the arms to hold me tight
and give me a sweet kiss goodnight

Parallel

We now stand parallel weaved together like a
perfect basket

Will there come a time that we crumble like stone

washed away, pushed apart from the shore

We spend our lives in struggle and joy
Shutting one door without locks or chains

Hoping that the new horizon will bring joy

We depend on the sun, the moon and the rain

We invest, we collect we reminisce
We call this living, a dream, hope, future

As the future fades we run for cover

Spread our wings, fly but sometimes dive
We indulge in emotions, frolic and faith

Loyal to love, to friends, to family
At least we try to be

The curtain is descending Who's there, who's
standing parallel to me

Pick Me

It's tough to sit here day after day
Hoping that someone will think I'm special

I try to wink, curl my nose, fluff my tail
And bark in a way that might entice you

I sit and stare and wonder what are they
looking for
Someone quiet, cute, tiny, big and brave

I know your kids would love me
I'm special and I really don't eat much

I don't bite, don't have fleas and I have a big
heart
My bark isn't loud but if a stranger is nearby I'll
protect you

It's tough to sit here day after day
I'm lonely and I just want a hug and to play

My paws are together see I pray please pick me
I just know that I could be your best friend.

Reminisce

I searched the crowd for faces
hoping you'd be there

I smell familiar flowers
remembering your hair

I watch the raindrops falling
as tears rolled down my face

I walk along the sandy shore
my heart begins to speak

I miss our time together
the clock no longer ticks

The sun will rise and set again
tomorrow's painful tricks

Save Me

Take me back in your arms, hold me close
and feel my pain

I'm sorry to deceive you, temptation is a sin,
you're the one that matters, cheating never wins

Deep inside your eyes, I know your missing me,
pride will only push you much further from me

Why was I so foolish, now I understand, stand
beside me one more time, I die without my man

No one else can move me, come satisfy my mind,
you're the link that's missing, return and
just be mine

Seasons

I love to walk in the snow and sink
down deep below
the cold seeps through my boots and my toes curl

I love to smell the flowers and watch the
bees at work
as the trees blossom with a parade of colors

I love to sit by the ocean and watch the
boats sail by
stroking to stay afloat in the warm water in July

I love to leaf peep through the woods
crunching sounds it feels so good

Separate Way

It wasn't meant to end this way,
That one would go the other stay

It's painful when one lover dies,
Not in body but inside

You start out close,
Passing time but one stands still so far behind

The guilt is strong and painful too,
The other feels alone and blue

It wasn't meant to end this way
But you stopped trying, fade away

The cloud got bigger it blocked my dreams,
You didn't get it so it seems

I'll say I'm sorry but not for me
My time has come, you've set me free

Silent One

How can I read you?
I'm not let in

I feel blinded
such a sin

So alone, don't you know?
a feeling so separate, so unknown

Deep inside a guessing game,
only you can release the pain

Maybe I am not the one,
can't let go but want to run

Hurt is there on both sides too
sharing, caring, feel so blue

Someday maybe you'll express
what it is that grows unrest?

Until then you won't disclose,
keep inside a broken rose

It makes me sad for I could be,
that person who can set you free

Sleep in Love

Can I tell you what is in my heart
How you fuel my day

That your touch heals my wounds
That your lips seal my emotions

We lay in a sea of blankets
As our pores release our love

Pressed together like sea urchins
floating in space above

Riding the foamy waves of daybreak
as the tide returns us to shore

We dream together, naughty lovers do
and touch a place your soul allows us to

Eyes closed we sleep entangled
as one person and we rest

So Hungry I Could Eat a Horse

Hors d'oeuvres a feast of crudités, canapés,
antipasto, dips and spreads
All of them go to your head

The waiting makes the wanting more
Escargot and shrimps galore

A giant plate of petit fours
Filled with jam, cream and much more

An elegant soup to touch your lips
Piece de resistance with garnished tips

Hot buttered rolls that drool and stick
Sour dough, focaccia, take your pick

A bowl of veggies garden fresh
Organic style seems the best

So hungry I could eat a horse
Would this happen BUT OF COURSE

Societies Girl

She colors her hair
No fat for me
societies pressure
of what I'm not to be

As thin as a model
my face oh so slight
to run on that treadmill
with all of her might

the picture they paint
of bones and slim waist
A fear that someday
there won't be a trace

The pressure is evil
affects us so young
to nourish my body
with nothing but sun

I walk down the catwalk with energy none
Calculate in my mind to eat a small crumb

My body does ache, my desire is strong,
I look in the mirror
I always look wrong.

Only to visit the bathroom each day
my hand down my throat
to release the pain

Soldier Boy

Another death, my heart is sad,
defeat, deceased, I can't relate

Patriotic I should be
but violence is not in me

Try to be hard and do what's right,
how can I when I'm scared to fight

I pretend to be like them,
but cry inside, ashamed again

Many times I'd pray for an end.
war and sadness are not my friend

My dreams of home and being free,
always seem so far from me

Life is hard and painful too,
my dreams may never come true

I must keep going so they say,
I hate war and continue to pray

No one understands me at all,
soldiers continue to fall

I look at him still lying there,
it makes me weak that they don't care

But I must continue on,
this is my world, it's not yet gone

Soul Mate

Your voice is strong
Your arms engulf me

Your hands tell your toil
Through life's passage

Your mind seldom rests
Your thoughts absorb your temple

Your eyes read every word
Your memory records each moment

You're so alive
You constantly thrive

You're all of this
and so much more

Special Little Boy

He sits apart from them
His silent eyes somewhere else
His mind races to a million places
Where does he go, I wonder
His smile melts my mood
His hugs make my day
He sits upon my lap
His mind caught in a trap
I worry, will he catch up
Will he understand my voice
The children laugh, he's different
I see him as the best
He's warm and funny
Energy in his steps
An artist, an author or VIP
No one can say for sure
For now he will stay in my arms
Safe and secure

Success

Success comes to those who persevere
In the shape of wealth, fame not fear

You must believe inside yourself
Put negative feelings on the shelf

Focus on your toughest you
Put away weakness and start anew

Forward direction, your soaring mind
Your intellect, create, divine

Acquaint yourself, a masterpiece
A new idea and plant a seed

Stomach in and chest held high
Proud until you touch the sky

Negative a dirty word
To think that way would be absurd

Success is failure turned upside down
Believe in you, a word profound

Sweet Baby Blue

Sweet seed inside
the longing now subsides

Dream warm thoughts
faceless masterpiece, magnificent warrior

Invade my body
with grace and dignity

Miracle of mine
I hear your laughter
Your tiny heart beats

How proud we will be
to teach you, hold you, even scold you

Sweet dreams grandbaby
Your Mom and Dad await you

The Beach

On the beach on a sunny day
Watch the children romp, scream and play

Bags with sand toys, castles to build
Dreading a drop of rain may spill

Where young lovers cuddle close
Umbrella, blanket, walk the shore
Hand in hand and wanting more

Seagulls screech a favorite tune
Summertime the warmth of June

Waves a roller coaster ride
Lifeguards do their job with pride

Blanket of sand a mile wide
Connecting people like the tide

On the beach our bodies glow
A place our heart will always know

The Darkness

Don't be afraid the shadows won't bite
Close your eyes and dream of the light

Chocolate is dark and you love that a lot
Dark is a color that makes round, round dots

Don't be afraid the shadows won't hurt
Dark is a color like God's pure brown earth

Some little girls have curly dark hair
bouncing in the air

The sun makes us darker healthy and new
So don't be afraid the shadows won't hurt YOU.

The Handkerchief

Something old I give to you,
long ago I held it too

Keep it close and dry your tears,
love and hope throughout the years

I held this on my wedding day,
my mother passed it on to me, now I pass it on to
you

with hope and prayer that your life be
filled with love and family eternally

The Longing

As a little girl I would dream of you
What would I call you, how would you look

Would you dance, would you sing
What mark would you make in this world

I wait each month for a sign of your beginning
Only to be disappointed once again

I spot a mother push a carriage
I imagine me steering you through life's wonders

I want to cuddle with you, clean a scraped knee,
dry a tear from your eye

The clock is ticking, I long to feel you move
inside me
Patient I must be

Gender doesn't matter
I would dress you in the finest lace
Or clean mud from your trousers and dirty face

I can teach you, travel the world
Make you the finest boy or girl

You would be my first
My love will cradle you
Keep you warm and safe

Please come to me
Precious seed of life

The Nightmare

You seem so real I suffocate, then choke
down that dark alley
Holding my breath, waiting for you to go away

Sometimes I walk on water, sink deep
below the ocean floor
Then rise and fly like an eagle to the moon

My mind is not my own as I enter into
another dimension
Faces twisted as I try to distinguish who they are

Like a bad movie on a low budget
portraying my life
A scary horror show, a bloody battle

Falling off a cliff, running away into the darkness
Alone in a place unknown to me

I scramble in bed, trying to find a safe haven
Trying to understand these visions in my head

I try to wake, then try to remember, play
it over again
What does it all mean, maybe Freud
could explain
They say "sweet dreams," I don't think so

The Ocean

Look out as far as your eyes will allow
Crystal blue, sea birds sing a summer tune

We ride the waves into the sun leaving our
worries behind

Feel the warmth of the sand as we crush prints
for others to trace
We walk the shore until our calves hurt,
brushing sand from our face

As the day lingers on we breathe the salty air not
having a care
Our bodies begin to bronze as our pores
beg for more

Soon the sun will set, savor each moment still
slightly wet

We will return another day and feel like
children, pretend to play

The ocean is my paradise, a place of wonder
feels so right

The Rocking Chair

A welcomed gift from long ago
it's cherry wood and sleek design

I placed you near the fireplace
and sat and rocked on cold, cold nights

I would sit and rock my child
sometimes fast like a carnival ride

Through fever, colds and sometimes flu
I would rock my baby too

Sitting there upon my chair
outside sun and crisp cool air

There were days that I would rock
just think of life and watch the clock

Years have passed some good some bad
I sit with gray hair feeling sad

No more babies sit upon me
It's their time now I've set them free

My chair is empty my heart is full
my rocking chair again will be
a grandchild upon my knee

The Soldier

The long, hot days are filled
with pain

We carry food, and watch
the rain

It hurts to see our comrades die,
we carry hurt, but never cry

Secret thoughts inside ourselves,
afraid of death but never tell

A heavy load upon our backs,
always watching our tracks

We carry thoughts of loved ones too
and dream of freedom to start anew

Sometimes we feel so alone
hearing hurt men moan

We carry a heavy load each day,
wire helmets, hats and clay

But the thing that we must do
is carry on and still hold true

The Sound of Laughter

It's free you know for all to share
The sound of laughter without a care

The magic that is in our soul
A pleasant sound to spread around

It comes from deep inside our chest
It makes us feel our very best

Just like a clown without a frown
We spread this joy from town to town

Some day if you should come upon
Give that person all your charm

A belly laugh to help him see
That laughter you can give for free

Never stop, a daily plight
Better laugh than to fight

The deepest laugh, Hyena style
A laugh you hear from mile to mile

The Wish

I wish that I could
feel for you and kiss the pain goodbye

I wish that I could
work for you until the day I die

I wish that I could
kiss you each and every day

I wish that I could
wake with you in the light of day

I wish that I could
bake for you, something sweeter than a cake

I wish that I could
pray for you to take away the ache

I wish that I could
think for you to give your mind a rest

I wish that I could
love you and always be the best

Time to Say Goodbye

She lies in her satin bed
So still, surrounded by loved ones

A single rose placed on her bosoms
Favorite dress of ivory and lace
Peaceful face, no pain, slender lips, eyes asleep

Angelic music played
Loved ones approaching in her honor

Say a prayer, wipe a tear, say goodbye
I close my eyes and you surround me

Did I say how much I loved you
How strong you were for me

I miss you already
Your stubbornness, your wit, your charm

Sleep in God's arms
Always feel my love

Time to say goodbye
Sweet dreams, beloved Mother of mine

Truth Speaking

I write to please the world
Let me tell you what my heart holds

To express my inner soul and how I feel
Share my feelings of life's wonders

God's creatures, the wonders of nature,
Life's beginning and the end

I won't always paint it pretty
Cold, hard facts are part of what I share

Listen deep within my words
No intention to scare, only to be fair

The ending of the world and its first beginning,
The thick and dirty air, the prophet
tells of sinning

Life's an open book, living moment to moment
Expecting much of nothing

Hoping that tomorrow will be here
Living this life in God's free air

Try to love each other
Try to understand

Share this earth together
The very best we can

Us

My body climbs higher
I dream of desire

Awaiting your touch
Hearts on fire

Pleasant poison
Dose by dose

Delicious delight
My body takes flight

Allowing your fingers
To chart your course

Breaking through
My private resource

We come together
Always as one

Sleep in my arms
Til morning comes

Vacation

Photographs of years gone by
The trips we took then said goodbye

Packing blankets, umbrellas and lotion galore
Your choice, destination, the Jersey Shore

A far-off island with palms to shade
White sand beaches that God has made

A jet soars in the sky to carry you, marry you,
honeymoon style
The perfect June, a silhouette, a lover's dream

Or pitch a tent, the chill of night, a warm fire,
feels so right
Singing songs from then and now in a circle
howling loud

Cruise the ocean day and night, salty water feels
all right
Feast and sing, friends galore enjoying always
wanting more

Take your pick; enjoy the ride, each vacation a
sense of pride

We Fly

Fireflies light my world with your touch
I get a thousand hugs, I'm your ladybug

You charm me with a kiss and a hug
Snuggle tight like a clam and a slug

You stroke my arm with magic dust
My skin, my seams begin to bust

Spider claws that dangle and pull
Web around me, I feel the thrill

We nest together, perched on high
Your touch so deep again we fly

When My Time Comes

Need not fear

Look to the light of eternity

Caress me in a peaceful state

I've dreamt of my final farewell

Place my hand on your precious face

I bow my head in your presence

May I look to you for warmth

This is more than I hoped for

My faith in you is what I long for

Am I worthy to stand beside you

Have I given enough to you and your earth

Whisper

Whisper, words, wisdom, love
Stroke, feel, touch caress my love

Guide, embrace, my silky form
Never leave a trace, you're gone

A secret place, tucked away
Where the water flows, the wind blows

A silent nest for two
Inspire me, fire me, devour me

Web me in your arms
Entangle me in your charm

Under the willow, four seasons pass
Crunch of snow, spring, summer grass

Hush, don't move, let it last
Whisper, whisper, here at last

Who Do I Belong To?

The wave took my parents away
Up to the Heaven's where they will stay

My country a ruin
My homeland is gone

Hear the cries from near and far
The air is clouded I'm no longer safe

Who will hold me and tuck me in
My old life no longer it's such a sin

Far away, someone loves me
Take me to a safe land

Hold my tiny hand
Tell me it will be all right

No one object, carry me today
On a big jet to a place far away

I welcome new parents
I'll miss the old

Someone must take me
To have and to hold

Why Can't I

A plane can fly through the clouds in the sky
why can't I

A bee can fly and buzz so free
why can't I

A kite can fly from a string so high
why can't I

A butterfly can fly on a colorful day
why can't I

A bird can fly with feathers away
why can't I

A helicopter can fly and spin and sway
why can't I

Mom do you know why?

Woman

I can be stronger than the mighty oak

I can be fragile as a porcelain teacup

I can cradle you in my arms until the pain
subsides

I can toil until I can no longer stand

I AM WOMAN

I can create life and support you until you're old

I can stand by you and love until eternity

I can care for you and never falter

I can hold you in my arms when you take your
last breath

I AM WOMAN

You Set me Free

You set me free without a tug
Just floated by without a hug

I glided, skated, danced away
Into a life that filled my day

No pull, no magnet, never tried
To catch me, hold me, give me pride

Encouragement to make me know
No gentle touch, no nights alone

You set me free, you never tried
To keep me safe, stand by your side

So now I'm free and so are you
No anger, just regrets for two

www.ingramcontent.com/pod-product-compliance
Lightning Source LLC
Chambersburg PA
CBHW061957040426
42447CB00010B/1792